10/92

GREAT MYSTERIES
Jack the Ripper
OPPOSING VIEWPOINTS®

Look for these and other exciting *Great Mysteries: Opposing Viewpoints* books:

GREAT MYSTERIES
Jack the Ripper
OPPOSING VIEWPOINTS®

by Katie Colby-Newton

Greenhaven Press, Inc.   P.O. Box 289009, San Diego, California 92198-0009

Library of Congress Cataloging-in-Publication Data

Colby-Newton, Katie, 1954-
    Jack the Ripper : opposing viewpoints / by Katie Colby-Newton.
        p.   cm. — (Great mysteries)
    Includes bibliographical references and index.
    Summary: Experts give differing views on the identity of the infamous murderer of nineteenth-century London.
    ISBN 0-89908-081-2
    1. Jack the Ripper Murders, London, England, 1888—Juvenile literature. [1. Jack the Ripper Murders, London, England, 1888. 2. Murder—England.] I. Title. II. Series: Great mysteries (Saint Paul, Minn.)
HV6535.G6L633   1990
364.1'523'092—dc20   90-3835
                                      CIP
                                      AC

To Anne,
for being in the right place
at the right time,
saying the right words.

"When men and women lose the sense of mystery, life will prove to be a gray and dreary business, only with difficulty to be endured."

Harold T. Wilkins, author of Strange Mysteries of Time and Space

Contents

Introduction

This book is written for the curious—those who want to explore the mysteries that are everywhere. To be human is to be constantly surrounded by wonderment. How do birds fly? Are ghosts real? Can animals and people communicate? Was King Arthur a real person or a myth? Why did Amelia Earhart disappear? Did history really happen the way we think it did? Where did the world come from? Where is it going?

Great Mysteries: Opposing Viewpoints books are intended to offer the reader an opportunity to explore some of the many mysteries that both trouble and intrigue us. For the span of each book, we want the reader to feel that he or she is a scientist investigating the extinction of the dinosaurs, an archaeologist searching for clues to the origin of the great Egyptian pyramids, a psychic detective testing the existence of ESP.

One thing all mysteries have in common is that there is no ready answer. Often there are *many* answers but none on which even the majority of authorities agrees. *Great Mysteries: Opposing Viewpoints* books introduce the intriguing views of the experts, allowing the reader to participate in their explorations, their theories, and their disagreements as they try to explain the mysteries of our world.

But most readers won't want to stop here. These *Great Mysteries: Opposing Viewpoints* aim to stimulate the reader's curiosity. Although truth is often impossible to discover, the search is fascinating. It is up to the reader to examine the evidence, to decide whether the answer is there—or to explore further.

"Penetrating so many secrets, we cease to believe in the unknowable. But there it sits nevertheless, calmly licking its chops."

H.L. Mencken, American essayist

Preface

"Murder!"

"Come, Watson, come! The game is afoot."

—Sir Arthur Conan Doyle

Imagine the city of London in 1888.

Imagine the evil-smelling alleyways and courtyards of Whitechapel in the East End. This area, the worst section of the city, has dark streets lighted only by gaslight. The lamps glow dimly yellow in the misty night. Walls, doorways, and windows are only fuzzily visible. Deep threatening shadows take over most of the walkways. The darkness and dirt can easily hide a murderer.

Imagine the constant ocean of noise in the slum: the bustle of delivery wagons rumbling on the way to market; the rattle of the carriages of wealthy men leaving prostitutes and drinking and gambling houses; the gruff conversations of workers on their way to and from jobs in the markets and slaughterhouses; the rattles, clangs, and whistles of a nearby train; the carousing of drunkards.

"Murder!" comes a cry from a Whitechapel courtyard. The chilling scream goes unheard. It is all part of the night noise. Jack the Ripper, the notorious murderer, escapes again, cloaked and invisible. The noise and the darkness swallow him up. Those few

Opposite: Cries of "Murder!" were not unusual in the poverty-stricken section of London known as Whitechapel. But the discovery of Jack the Ripper's first victim signalled a whole new kind of terror.

who are searching for him are baffled by his ability to vanish without a trace. Few Londoners are left unafraid of the phantom killer.

The Search Goes On

More than a hundred years have passed since the gruesome Whitechapel murders were committed by Jack the Ripper. The infamous killer's identity is still unknown. Yet the search for him goes on.

Violent death was common in Whitechapel and the other poor sections of London at the end of the nineteenth century. Yet these particular murders unnerved all of London, rich and poor. Nothing quite like them had ever happened before. In fact, Jack the Ripper, murderer of lowly prostitutes, managed to shake the entire English nation. The murders challenged England's prim and lofty ideas about human nature.

The original Metropolitan Police reports of the Whitechapel murders are contained in three large manila envelopes in a dilapidated cardboard box at Scotland Yard. The three envelopes were marked "Victims," "Suspects," and "Letters." The files were marked to be sealed until 1992; however, they were opened in the 1970s. Many seekers of the identity of Jack the Ripper hoped these secret files would reveal the killer. But they did not.

The British Home Office secret files also contained numerous reports about the murders, most from local police. The only other remaining information is found in newspaper accounts from the time. They give conflicting information.

Experts say that much evidence has been destroyed, either accidentally or on purpose. Some was lost during the bombing of London in World War II. Some was lost by mismanagement. Some was deliberately destroyed to save space or, according to some people, to protect an important person's identity. The scanty evidence, however, has not kept people, then and now, from speculating on the identity of Jack the Ripper. Millions of words have been written; unnumbered theories have been advanced; a multitude of names and faces have been recorded in the search for the bloodchilling killer. But so far, no certain answers have been found. Even Jack's motive remains a question.

Who Was the Ripper?

Some Ripperologists—those who study Jack the Ripper—say that the killer was nothing more than a crazed madman, no different from the occasional psychopaths we read about in today's daily newspapers. These experts suggest that the case gained so much notoriety because these were the first highly publicized crimes of their kind.

Some experts believe the murderer was an unbalanced man who sought to bring attention to the terrible plight of the poor. He committed crimes so horrible that public attention would be drawn not only to the victims but to the living conditions of all the poor people in this squalid section of London.

Still a third group of Ripperologists points to the police handling of the evidence. Why would the police seal the files of five unimportant prostitutes? Why was some evidence destroyed? These Ripperologists suggest that the sealed files must mean that something very important, possibly dangerous to the nation, was being covered up. Perhaps the killer was a very important government figure—even a member of the royal family. Perhaps the murders were committed to protect someone.

The mystery of these brutal crimes is as perversely fascinating today as it was the year they happened. Who was Jack the Ripper and why did he do what he did?

POLICE NOTICE.

TO THE OCCUPIER.

On the mornings of Friday, 31st August, Saturday 8th, and Sunday, 30th September, 1888, Women were murdered in or near Whitechapel, supposed by some one residing in the immediate neighbourhood. Should you know of any person to whom suspicion is attached, you are earnestly requested to communicate at once with the nearest Police Station.

Metropolitan Police Office,
30th September, 1888.

Printed by M'Corquodale & Co. Limited, " The Armoury," Southwark.

By posting notices like this one around the city, the police hoped to obtain some clue to the baffling murders.

One

The Scene of the Crime

Life in the East End of London in the 1880s was almost unbelievably poor. Calling this area the East End is more polite than calling it the Back Side or the Hind End. But that is what it was: a huge dumping ground for the outcasts of humanity.

The population of the East End was dense and the poverty intense. It was a filthy place. Slum buildings lined crooked, narrow streets. The people living there lacked such minor comforts as warm, dry rooms and adequate food and clothing. They had little or no education. They were deprived of even the most basic need—the sense that society cared about them.

The Poor of London

About 900,000 people lived in the East End in the 1880s. Whitechapel, a section of the East End, held about 80,000 people. Charles Booth, a journalist from that time, divided the population of this poor area into three groups. At the highest level were the "working poor." They held regular jobs at incredibly low wages, usually between eleven and eighteen shillings per week. Even with their jobs, they could not make ends meet. They lived in a state of chronic want. Next came the "very poor." With only occasional employment at some task or other, they earned even less than the working poor. At the lowest level were those who

Opposite: People and animals were crowded together in the Whitechapel slums.

Unemployment was high among these unskilled and uneducated inhabitants of the East End. This picture shows victims of evictions crowded into an alley.

were rarely employed, the "occasional labourers, loafers, and semi-criminals." The lives of the poorest two groups are painful to imagine.

At least 11,000 people in Whitechapel were unemployed. This figure included the *dossers* (people who rented a bed or a space in a rooming establishment called a doss) and the homeless who slept in doorways, garbage heaps, and public restrooms. Charles Booth recorded, "They render no useful service, they create no wealth; more often than not they destroy it. They degrade whatever they touch, and as individuals are perhaps incapable of improvement." The prospects for their children were bleak. Often these children were left to fend for themselves on the street or were crowded into pauper schools where they could try to get brief, basic educations.

Those who were employed often were physically and mentally unfit to do their work because they ate so irregularly. They labored for such small amounts of money that they lived not day to day but hour to hour. Food was bought to be eaten immediately. Booth made note of one family who, like many others, bought nothing until it was needed. They went to the store as we go to our cupboards and shelves: "Twice a day they buy tea, or three times a day if they make it so often; in thirty-five days they made seventy-two purchases of tea." All those purchases were for "a pinch of tea," enough for a cup or two. This family made seventy-seven purchases of sugar during the same period. They had nowhere to store a larger quantity even if they had the money to buy it.

Living Day-to-Day

Most of these people lived on a day-to-day basis in lodging houses called dosses. Rooms in these houses were rented to families for eight pence a night. A survey of the area, taken in 1883, showed that three-quarters of these people lived with their whole family in one room. Most indicated that they shared the room with from five to nine other people. Each room usually held only one bed. The children slept on rags or straw on the floor. The single toilet in the building was on the ground floor. Most families used chamber pots which were infrequently emptied—into the yard. A single standing pipe in the alley often provided the only water for the entire building. Vermin—rats and bugs—infested the walls of most of these houses.

Fewer than half the children born in the East End survived to the age of five. They suffered from lack of food and from exposure to the elements. Because of their deprivation, they were physically and mentally underdeveloped. Booth reported, "One tenth of elementary school children were estimated later to be mentally defective, or unnaturally dull. Children frequently came to school crying with hunger and fell off their seats from exhaustion. In winter they could not learn because they were too cold."

A Whitechapel family squeezes all of its living and working into a single room.

Many London lodging houses, like this one, forced its tenants to sleep on hard, dank floors.

The Bitter Cry of Outcast London by Andrew Mearns dramatically paints this picture of the lives of the poor:

> In one cellar a sanitary inspector reports finding a father, mother, three children, and four pigs! In another room a missionary found a man ill with smallpox and his wife recovering from her eighth confinement [pregnancy], and the children running about half naked and covered with dirt. Here are seven people living in one underground kitchen, and a little dead child lying in the same room. Elsewhere is a poor widow, her three children, and a child who had been dead thirteen days. Her husband, who was a cabman, had shortly before committed suicide . . . .
>
> Here [in another room] is a mother who turns her children into the streets in the early evening because she lets her room for immoral purposes until long after midnight, when the poor little wretches creep back again if they have not found some miserable shelter elsewhere . . . .
>
> In many cases matters are made worse by the unhealthy occupations followed by those who dwell in these habitations. Here you are choked as you enter by the air laden with particles of the superfluous fur pulled from the skins of rabbits, rats, dogs, and other small animals in their

preparations for the furrier. Here the smell of paste and of drying match-boxes, mingling with other sickly odors, overpowers you . . . . Even when it is possible to do so the people seldom open their windows, but if they did it is questionable whether much would be gained, for the external air is scarcely less heavily charged with poison than the atmosphere within.

Lodging-house police inspected the dosses weekly, but landlords had enough time to prepare their houses. Conditions even in this "cleaned-up" state were grim. One sergeant reported, "The place was swarming with vermin, large blocks of creeping things having been taken out of the walls and ceilings. The bedsteads and bedding were also swarming with insects, and disgusting in the extreme."

Most dwellers of these houses were employed, if at all, at unskilled odd jobs. The little money they earned was spent on liquor or on basic food such as bread, margarine, tea, and sugar. Often there was not enough left over for a room at night. It was not unusual for whole families to sleep leaning against a building. It was a brutal and rootless existence.

Workhouses provided mindless, often pointless, work which the poor did in exchange for a bed and a meal.

Workhouses

For those permanently unemployed, or unable to pay for a night's lodging, there was another choice—workhouses. They offered the homeless a place to stay and something to eat in exchange for labor. The work was usually mindless and needless. For example, someone in a workhouse might pound rocks into dust to be hauled away.

The American writer Jack London wrote a vivid account of his 1902 stay in a workhouse. His assigned task was to go to the Whitechapel infirmary (sick ward) to search for edible food. Men from the workhouse collected food not eaten by the sick and scraped it into sacks. London's job was to haul the sacks down five flights of stairs where they would be emptied into garbage cans and sprinkled with a disinfectant. The men of the workhouse received their portion of food from this container.

The workhouse offered survival and little else.

This then is the scene in the East End of London in 1888. Poverty, degradation, desperation, and despair filled the streets. When Jack the Ripper started his dirty work, he became one more horror for these poor people to face.

"The British race was enfeebling itself and dividing into two classes, a master race and a ghetto race."

Andrew Sinclair,
Jack: A Biography of Jack London

"There was very little alienation in Victorian London or Liverpool. The poor might wish they had a better place in society, but they didn't feel alienated from it."

Author and Ripperologist
Donald Rumbelow,
Jack the Ripper:
The Complete Casebook

Opposite: People of all ages were forced to stay out on the dark, forbidding streets if they had no money for a night's lodging.

Two

Jack and His Victims

The myths surrounding the Whitechapel murders are widespread and numerous. These myths contradict each other concerning the number of victims and where they were killed. The different versions have Jack the Ripper responsible for as many as twenty or as few as three or four gruesome murders. They supposedly took place not only in London but in towns all over England and even on the European continent. The killer was said to be disguised and dangerous. Stories of his bloody deeds were told (and still are!) to frighten little children—"Watch out! The Ripper's lurkin'!"

Despite the many versions, most Ripperologists agree with Sir Melville Macnaghten: The madman (or woman) committed five murders for certain.

Sir Melville Macnaghten joined Scotland Yard as assistant chief constable with the Criminal Investigation Department (known as the CID) in 1889, a year after the murders took place. His notes are among the best known of all the Ripper documents. They were in the confidential "Victims" file at Scotland Yard. Macnaghten's notes on the number of victims are specific:

The Illustrated Police News was one of many sensational tabloids that kept the populace informed about the deeds of Jack the Ripper.

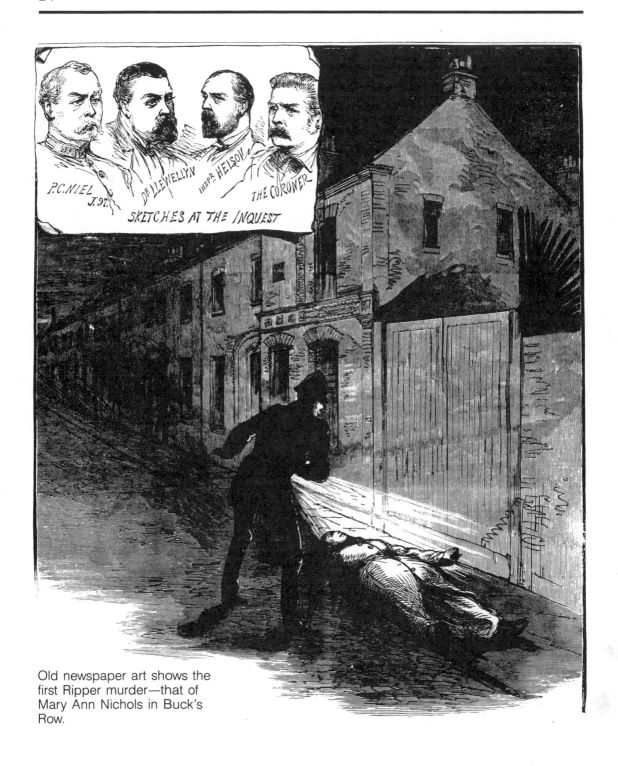

P.C. NIEL. J.97.

DR LLEWELLYN

INSPR HELSON

THE CORONER

SKETCHES AT THE INQUEST

Old newspaper art shows the first Ripper murder—that of Mary Ann Nichols in Buck's Row.

Now the Whitechapel Murderer had 5 victims and 5 victims only.---his murders were

(i) 31st Aug '88. Mary Ann Nichols---at Buck's Row---who was found with her throat cut---& with (slight) stomach mutilation.

(ii) 8th Sept '88. Annie Chapman---Hanbury Street: throat cut---stomach & [other mutilations]. . . .

(iii) 30th Sept '88. Elizabeth Stride---Berner's Street: throat cut, but nothing in shape of mutilation attempted, & on same date Catherine Eddowes---Mitre Square, throat cut, & very bad mutilation, both of face & stomach.

(iv) 9th November. Mary Jane Kelly---Miller's Court, throat cut, and the whole of the body mutilated in the most ghastly manner.

The victims file, neatly tied with pink tape, also contains individual case files with notes made at the scene of each crime. Inspector Frederick George Abberline, a detective with Scotland Yard, collected all of the reports and combined them. Some Ripperologists say his reports are the most accurate and valuable materials on the Whitechapel murders. Others say they are not. Curiously, Abberline's notes indicate causes of death and states of the bodies but leave out some of the clues left by the murderer. Many are mentioned in newspaper articles and journalists' notes that are not in the police files. Information from these various sources helps round out the picture of the murders and the victims.

What Is Known About the Victims?

The first certain victim of Jack the Ripper was Mary Ann Nichols. Her body was found by a passer-by, Charles Cross, around 3:15 a.m. on August 31, 1888, in Buck's Row, a dark side street in Whitechapel. Constable John Neil was on duty in the area and had passed that spot at half-hour intervals all night. He came upon the body shortly after Cross left to find

"Michael Harrison must claim the current record for the greatest number of victims attributed to the Ripper by a modern writer. He has suggested that ten women were killed by the Ripper."

Authors Martin Howells
and Keith Skinner,
The Ripper Legacy

"The Whitechapel murderer committed five murders, and—to give the devil his due—no more."

Assistant Chief Constable
Melville Macnaghten,
Days of My Years

Scotland Yard Inspector Sir Melville Macnaghten. He was convinced there were only five Ripper killings.

the police. It was on the footway on its back against some gates leading into a stable yard.

There was little blood at the scene, which was odd considering the severity of the woman's wounds. Her throat had been cut as had her abdomen. A local doctor named Llewellyn pronounced the woman dead, and her body was taken to the mortuary.

The description of the victim, taken from the police report, reads,

> age about 45; length 5 ft 2 or 3; complexion dark; hair dark brown turning grey; eyes brown. . . .
>
> Dress; brown ulster, 7 large brass buttons, . . . brown lindsey frock, grey woollen petticoats [Inspector Abberline recorded that these petticoats were stenciled "Lambeth Workhouse" where the police went for information to identify the body.], flannel drawers, white chest flannel, brown stays, black ribbed woollen stockings, men's spring-sided boots, . . . black straw bonnet, trimmed with black velvet.

Abberline's report added the victim's name, address, and background:

> Former inmate [of Lambeth Workhouse] named Mary Ann Nichols . . . . wife of William Nichols of 37 Coburg Street, Old Kent Road, . . . from whom she had been separated about nine years through her drunken and immoral habits, . . . inmate at various workhouses. . . . In May of this year she left Lambeth Workhouse and entered the service of Mr Cowdry. . . . She remained there until 12th July when she absconded stealing various articles of wearing apparel. A day or two after, she became a lodger at 18 Thrawl Street, Spitalfields, a common lodging house, and at another common lodging house at 56 Flower & Dean Street up until the night of the murder.

Mary Ann Nichols had last been seen at 18 Thrawl Street at 1:40 a.m. She had told the manager of the lodging house that she had no money for a bed but

A newspaper of the day summarizes events in several of the Ripper murders.

to save her one. She went out to try to get the money. She was drunk when she left. Ellen Holland, a lodger of the same house, saw her, still drunk, at 2:30 a.m. at the corner of Osborn Street and Whitechapel Road. She requested that Nichols return with her to the lodging house. Nichols declined and continued down Whitechapel Road, headed in the direction where her body was later found, about a half-mile away. Abberline recorded that no one else had seen Mary Ann Nichols until her body was found. He also stated, "Inquiries were made in every conceivable quarter with a view to trace the murderer but not the slightest clue can at present be obtained."

Anne Chapman

The Ripper's second certain victim was found eight days later. At 6:10 a.m. on September 8, 1888, Police Inspector Joseph Chandler was called to Hanbury Street. There lay another woman's body. Inspector Abberline recorded that there was no doubt the same person had committed both murders.

Inspector Chandler reported that at No. 29 Hanbury Street, in the backyard, he found "a woman lying on her back, dead, left arm resting on left breast,

Hanbury Street, Spitalfields, where Jack the Ripper and his second victim, Annie Chapman, passed.

legs drawn up." Her abdomen had been cut and part of her intestines placed above her right shoulder. Her throat was "cut deeply from left and back in a jagged manner right around the throat." Blood was found on the wall and fence close to the body.

A police surgeon, Dr. Phillips, pronounced the victim dead and the body was taken to the Whitechapel mortuary.

Inspector Chandler's report described the victim:

Annie Siffey [also known as Chapman], age 45; length 5 ft; complexion fair; hair wavy, dark brown; eyes blue; two teeth deficient in lower jaw, large thick nose.

Dress: black figured jacket, brown bodice, black skirt, lace boots, all old and dirty.

The body was identified by Timothy Donovan, manager of the lodging house at 35 Dorset Street, where Anne Chapman had lived most recently. Donovan reported that on September 8 at 1:45 a.m., he had seen her eating potatoes in the kitchen. She had been drunk and without money for a bed. When Donovan refused to extend her credit, she left, saying she would be back soon with some money.

Dr. Phillips's personal notes contained an important list of clues that were not in the police report. The murderer had placed several articles around the murder scene. He left a piece of muslin fabric, a comb, and a paper case close to the body. He laid two rings he had taken from his victim's fingers, some pennies, and two new farthings (coins worth one-fourth penny each) at the foot of the body. At the head he placed an envelope and a piece of paper containing two pills. The back of the envelope was printed with the seal of the Sussex military regiment and the front with the letter *M* and a post office stamp. A leather apron, or part of one (accounts vary), soaked with water, was lying about two feet from a nearby water faucet. The apron was, for a time, considered by the investigators to be a major clue. The rings, coins, envelope, and other items were forgotten.

Why did the murderer leave these clues? They looked carefully placed, not carelessly dropped. Were they part of a strange ritual? Did they contain a message about the murderer's identity? Over the decades since the murders, many people have tried to answer these questions with differing results, some of which will be examined later in this book.

The Double Murder

Three weeks after Anne Chapman's death, the mysterious Whitechapel murderer struck again. This time he killed two victims on the same night. The murders took place in the early morning hours of September 30, 1888.

The first occurred on Berner Street behind a workmen's club. The *London Times* described the court at the end of the street where the body was found as being in "absolute darkness." On October 19, Chief Inspector Donald Swanson presented his report about the crime. In it he wrote,

> I beg to report that the following are the particulars respecting the murder of Elizabeth Stride on the morning of 30 September 1888.---
>
> 1 a.m. 30th Sept. A body of a woman was found with the throat cut, but not otherwise mutilated, by Louis Diemschutz (secretary to the Socialist Club) inside the gates of Dutfield's yard in Berner Street, Commercial Road East, who gave information to the police. [Police Constable] Lamb proceeded with him to the spot and sent for Drs Blackwell and Phillips.
>
> 1.10 a.m. Body examined by the doctors mentioned who pronounced life extinct, the position of the body was as follows:---lying on left side, left arm extended from elbow, cachous [small candies] lying in her hand, right arm over stomach, back of hand and inner surface of wrist dotted with blood, legs drawn up, knees fixed, feet close to wall, body still warm, silk handkerchief round

A newspaper artist drew the site of the "barbarous murder" of Annie Chapman.

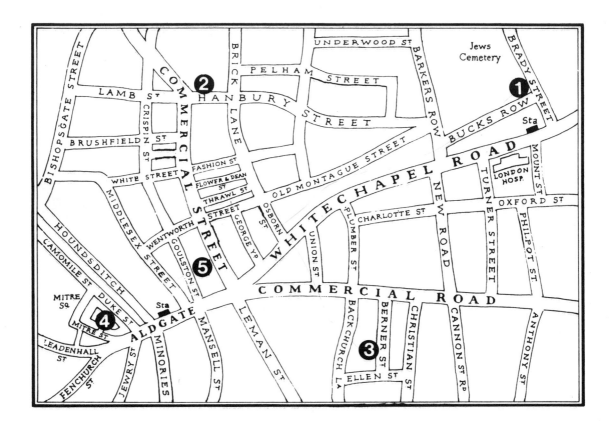

A map showing the sites of the five certain Ripper killings. Note that they form a rough cross pattern. Some Ripperologists have thought this pattern was a clue to the killer. One explanation is that Jack was a religious fanatic determined to cleanse the world of prostitutes.

throat, slightly torn corresponding to the angle of right jaw, throat deeply gashed and below the right angle apparent abrasion of skin about an inch and a quarter in diameter.

Search was made in the yard but no instrument found.

This report leaves out a possible clue reported by two newspapers. On October 1, 1888, the *Times* stated, "in her right hand were tightly clasped some grapes." The *Evening News* also stated that Stride's right hand was clutching grapes. The *News* even found a witness who claimed he had sold grapes to a man he had seen with Stride. This clue was dismissed as untrue at the inquests, but it was positively verified. The police files contain a report stating, "Two private enquiry men [detectives] . . . upon searching a drain in the yard found a grape stem which was amongst the other matter swept from the yard after its examination by the police." Were these grapes the clue that could have solved the mystery of Jack the Ripper if the police had taken it seriously?

Three Quarters of a Mile and Ten Minutes

The scene of the second murder of the night was Mitre Square, three quarters of a mile away, a ten-minute walk from Berner Street. Catherine Eddowes, the victim, was found at 1:45 a.m. by Constable Watkins. Her face was mutilated almost beyond recognition. A portion of her nose had been cut off, the lobe of her right ear nearly severed, and her face slashed. Her throat had been cut, her abdomen severely slashed, and one kidney had been removed. The brutal killer had apparently either done his gruesome and skilled work in only a few moments or, more likely, had killed Eddowes in one of the nearby empty buildings and then placed the body in the alley.

Chief Inspector Swanson reported that both at 1:30 and 2:20 the constable on duty had seen nothing suspicious in the vicinity of the murder. However, at 2:55 a.m., the constable discovered a piece of blood-stained apron at the bottom of a staircase. Above it on the wall was chalked the puzzling sentence, "The JUWES are not the men That Will be Blamed for nothing." Inspector Swanson's report also stated that Dr. Brown and Dr. Phillips had done a post mortem autopsy. Their report noted that the murder could have been committed by "a hunter, a butcher, a student in surgery, or a properly qualified surgeon." Further, Swanson reported,

> The result of the City Police enquiries were as follows:--- . . . Catherine Eddowes . . . had been locked up for drunkenness at Billingsgate Street Police Station at 8:45 p.m. 29th and being sober was discharged at 1 a.m. 30th. . . . It was found that there did not exist amongst her relations

"The murderer had pulled off some brass rings which the victim had been wearing and these, together with some trumpery articles which had been taken from her pockets, were placed carefully at the victim's feet."

Journalist Oswald Allen,
Pall Mall Gazette,
September 8, 1888

"Two things were missing from the body. Chapman's rings, which had not been found, and the uterus, which had been taken from the abdomen."

Coroner Wynne Baxter, in his postmortem remarks on Annie Chapman's murder, September 26, 1888 [taken from Stephen Knight's *Jack the Ripper*]

or friends the slightest pretext for a motive to commit murder.

The Final Victim

The headlines of the *Illustrated Police News* on November 9, 1888, announced what everyone had feared: ANOTHER WHITECHAPEL HORROR, MORE REVOLTING MUTILATION THAN EVER.

Mary Kelly's turn had come. She had been brutally murdered in her room, number 13, Miller's Court. As with the other victims, her throat had been cut. Her body was mutilated more severely than all the others. This time the killer had also removed some of the skin from her legs.

In a desperate effort to identify the fiendish murderer, a photographer took pictures of the victim's eyes. Many people of that time believed that in cases of violent death, the last images seen by the victim were permanently recorded on the retina of the eye. Photographs of them might reveal the killer's identity.

Left: Millers Court in Dorset Street where the body of Mary Kelly, the Ripper's fifth victim, was found. Right: Mitre Square, where the fourth victim, Elizabeth Stride, was found.

A newspaper drawing shows Catherine Eddowes and a man who may have been her killer.

Unfortunately, these photos did not tell who Jack the Ripper was.

Inspector Abberline's handwritten reports provide the scanty official information about Mary Kelly's death. There is little information about the crime scene. Abberline mainly recorded statements made by people who knew the victim (the boarding house landlord at 26 Dorset Street, the man she lived with, the woman she had lived with, and friends) and people who had seen the victim on the night of the murder. Kelly had been seen talking with a man who had a mustache, was wearing a hat, and was carrying a small, long leather bag.

Mary Kelly was the last certain victim of the Whitechapel murderer. Curiously, most Ripperologists note, there were lengthy official files and long inquests on the murders of Mary Ann Nichols and Anne Chapman. Much less information was recorded about the third and fourth victims and almost nothing was

"I am almost tempted to disclose the identity of the murderer....But no public benefit would result from such a course."

Inspector Robert Anderson,
The Lighter Side of My Official Life

"The truth was that none of the evidence or understanding available at the time of the murders was conclusive enough to allow a finger to be pointed at any particular group of people, let alone a specific individual."

Authors Martin Howells and
Keith Skinner, *The Ripper Legacy*

recorded on Mary Kelly. What was the reason for this? What was Scotland Yard doing about the most horrific murders on record? Why was there so little official information? Was there by now a government cover-up? Were the police bored with the case and consequently careless?

Letters from Jack

The murderer was not content to do his bloody deeds and skulk away into the darkness. He also felt a need to brag about them. During the course of the investigations, numerous letters purporting to be from the killer were sent to the newspapers and the police. Scotland Yard's "Letters" file contains hundreds of such letters. Only a very few of them, however, are thought to actually have come from Jack. Most came from cranks who got a perverse pleasure out of taunting the police and making crude jokes about the murders.

One of the early letters gave Jack his name. Experts debate whether this letter was actually written by the murderer. But it clearly refers to related events. ("Leather Apron" refers to the arrest of a suspect named John Pizer following Anne Chapman's murder. He was a boot finisher who wore a leather apron while doing his work and was consequently nicknamed "Leather Apron." He was held briefly by the police and then released.) The letter was received at the Central News Agency on Thursday, September 27, 1888.

> Dear Boss,
> I keep on hearing the police have caught me, but they won't fix me just yet. I have laughed when they look so clever and talk about being on the right track. The joke about Leather Apron gave me real fits.
> I am down on whores and I shan't quit ripping them till I do get buckled. Grand work the last job was. I gave the lady no time to squeal. How can

they catch me now? I love my work and want to start again. You will soon hear of me with my funny little games.

I saved some of the proper red stuff in a ginger beer bottle over the last job to write with but it went thick like glue and I can't use it. Red ink fits enough, I hope ha ha.

The next job I do I shall clip the lady's ears off and send them to the police officers just for jolly wouldn't you? Keep this letter. I will do a bit more work, then give it out straight. My knife is nice and sharp. I want to get to work right away if I get a chance. Good luck.

Yours truly
Jack the Ripper

Most Ripperologists agree that Mary Kelly was the fifth and final victim of Jack the Ripper's lethal knife.

The murderer, if indeed he was the author of the letter, had named himself and in so doing made himself unforgettable. Tom Cullen's book, *When London Walked in Terror*, tells how this nickname might have developed. "Jack" was a popular name for many famous criminals of the past—Jack Sheppard, Spring-Heeled Jack, Sixteen-Stringed Jack, Three-Fingered Jack, and Slippery Jack are a few. "High Rip" gangs mostly robbed or assaulted prostitutes. Combining the two gives us "Jack the Ripper."

Only two days after the signature letter, "Jack" sent a note postmarked in Liverpool, another British city. It warned that the murderer would soon commit another crime:

Beware, I shall be at work on the first and second in Minories [an area in the East End] at twelve midnight and I give the authorities a good chance, but there is never a policeman near when I am at work.

Indeed, on September 29, he killed Elizabeth Stride and Catherine Eddowes. The next day, before the killings were publicized in the newspaper, "Jack" sent the following note to the Central News Agency:

I was not codding dear old Boss when I gave you the tip. You'll hear about Saucy Jack's work

One of the hundreds of letters the police received from people claiming to be the notorious killer. The writer signs himself "Jack the Ripper."

The letter which Mr. Lusk, head of the Vigilance Committee, received along with a gruesome package—a kidney!

tomorrow. Double even this time. Number one squealed a bit. Couldn't finish straight off. Had not time to get ears for police. Thanks for keeping last letter back till I got to work again.

JACK THE RIPPER

Beside the words was a bloody thumbprint.

Only the killer could have known about the failed attempt to cut off one of Anne Chapman's ears.

A Mr. Lusk of Alderney Road was head of the local Vigilance Committee, a neighborhood group that tried to reduce crime in various ways. Lusk often aided the police in the search for clues in the Ripper case.

On the fifteenth of October he received a grisly package. He found the contents alarming enough to deliver them to Dr. Openshaw, the curator of the London Hospital Museum, who pronounced them to be a human kidney. In the report to the police, Dr. Openshaw suggested that the kidney could have been taken from any dead person upon whom a post mortem had been done for any cause, by a student, or by a dissecting room attendant. The kidney, or rather a portion of the kidney, was accompanied by a letter:

Mr. Lusk, head of the Vigilance Committee.

From hell

Mr Lusk
   Sir
   I send you half the Kidne I took from one woman prasarved it for you tother piece I fried and ate it was very nise. I may send you the bloody knif that took it out if you only wate a whil longer
   signed   Catch me when
           you can
            Mishter Lusk

The End

Was this letter from the real killer? Despite the broad hints about locations, details from the crimes, and so forth, neither this nor any of the other letters offered the police enough help to catch Jack. He began his reign of terror suddenly, killing and mutilating these five women—and maybe others. But just as suddenly as he began, he disappeared. The killings stopped. Many people assumed Jack the Ripper was dead. But who was he?

Three

What Kind of Person Was Jack the Ripper?

What kind of person could have committed the unspeakably horrible crimes of Jack the Ripper? At the time the Whitechapel murders were committed and in the years since, many experts have accused suspects or have said they know the identity of the famous killer. But to this day there is no agreement and no proof.

A hundred years ago, as today, the police sometimes created psychological profiles of unknown criminals. From the way the crimes are committed, the types of victims, and the clues left at the scene, experts are able to make "educated guesses" as to the type of person or persons who would commit such crimes. In many cases, when the criminal is caught, he or she fits the psychological profile remarkably well.

Psychology was an infant science at the time of the Ripper killings. Even so, police experts were able to see patterns and make predictions about the characters of criminals.

Dr. Bond's Post Mortem Notes

In November of 1888, Dr. Thomas Bond performed the post mortem examination on the body of

Suspects in the Ripper killings were numerous. Here, local Vigilance
Committee members are suspicious of an immigrant.

"The injuries had been made by someone who had considerable anatomical knowledge and skill. There were no meaningless cuts."

Coroner Wynne Baxter, in his postmortem comments on Annie Chapman's murder, September 26, 1888

"In each case the mutilation was inflicted by a person who had no scientific nor anatomical knowledge. In my opinion he does not even possess the technical knowledge of a butcher."

Dr. Thomas Bond, in the findings of his postmortem on Mary Jane Kelly [quoted in *The Ripper Legacy*]

Mary Kelly, the Ripper's fifth victim. Based on his results and what he knew about the other four Ripper murders, he drew several important conclusions. Some of his conclusions have been challenged. Nevertheless, his observations provided important information for the police in their search for this ruthless killer.

Here are excerpts from Dr. Bond's notes.

1. All five murders were no doubt committed by the same hand. . . .

2. . . . The women must have been lying down when murdered and in every case the throat was cut first. [Later experts thought the women had been strangled first because there was relatively little blood at the scenes of the crimes.]. . .

4. In all the cases there appears to be no evidence of struggling and the attacks were probably so sudden and made in such a position that the woman could neither resist nor cry out. . . .

6. The murderer would not necessarily be splashed or deluged with blood, but his hands and arms must have been covered and parts of his clothing must certainly have been smeared with blood.

7. . . . In all the murders the object was mutilation.

8. In each case the mutilation was inflicted by a person who had no scientific nor anatomical knowledge. In my opinion he does not even possess the technical knowledge of a butcher or horse slaughterer or any person accustomed to cut up dead animals. [Other experts, including Inspector Macnaghten, thought the Ripper had a good deal of anatomical knowledge. For that reason, the police sought doctors and butchers as prime suspects.] . . .

Here are some keys to the killer's physical and mental character.

10. The murderer must have been a man of physical strength and of great coolness and daring. There is no evidence that he had an accomplice. He must in my opinion be a man subject

During the Ripper scare, the police questioned many vagrants.

to attacks of Homicidal and erotic mania. . . . It is of course possible that the Homicidal impulse may have developed from a revengeful or brooding condition of the mind, or that religious mania may have been the original disease but I do not think either hypothesis is likely. The murderer in external appearance is quite likely to be a quiet inoffensive looking man, probably middle-aged and neatly and respectably dressed. I think he must be in the habit of wearing a cloak or overcoat or he could hardly have escaped notice in the streets if the blood on his hands or clothes were visible.

11. Assuming the murderer to be such a person as I have just described, he would be solitary and eccentric in his habits, also he is most likely

The police actively patrolled the streets and alleys during the Ripper's
reign of terror, but they never managed to nab him.

to be a man without regular occupation, but with some small income or pension. He is possibly living among respectable persons who have some knowledge of his character and habits and who may have grounds for suspicion that he isn't quite right in his mind at times. Such persons would probably be unwilling to communicate suspicions to the Police for fear of trouble or notoriety.

This report, sent to Inspector Robert Anderson of Scotland Yard, provided fodder for the police in their search for the killer. But, as with all psychological profiles, it was conjecture—not fact and not evidence.

Modern Explanations

In the decades since the Whitechapel murders, many other experts have added to and refined the psychological profile of the murderer and have tried to explain how he became the psychopath he was. Colin Wilson, a famous British criminal psychologist, wrote the introduction to Donald Rumbelow's book *Jack the Ripper: The Complete Casebook*. Wilson makes some educated guesses about the murderer and about the causes of his criminal obsession. He explains how the thought process behind such crimes develops and explodes into the violence perpetrated by Jack the Ripper.

Wilson states that the Victorians, the people living during the reign of Queen Victoria of England, were shocked by these Ripper murders. These sensational killings and mutilations were different from anything that had happened before. Violent murders were not infrequent in London, but not murders like these. Most crimes in Victorian London were economic in origin, and there were plenty of them: robberies, murders, assaults, burglaries, and rapes. Most were the result of poverty and economic inequities.

Wilson suggests that the Industrial Revolution might be the key to what started a change in society, the change that made it possible for a Jack the Ripper to develop. The Industrial Revolution brought a dramatic change in the structure of people's lives. Society became industrial instead of agricultural. People left their small communities and farms. They moved to crowded cities and took hard jobs in polluted factories, manufacturing all kinds of goods. The Industrial Revolution in England took shape from about the mid-1700s to mid-1800s.

Wilson refers to the theories of Sir Arthur Keith, author of *A New Theory of Human Evolution*. Sir Arthur stated that society has two codes of conduct. The first is the code of amity, or love between the

The Industrial Revolution changed the world. It brought numerous benefits, but it also brought many evils. The new industries exploited poor workers, including many children, with long hours, low wages, and dangerous conditions.

members of society. It can be compared to patriotism or team spirit. It is the bonding, the caring, the love between people who share a common culture. The second code is the code of enmity, or hatred of society. The people who follow this code feel outside of and apart from the group. Before the Industrial Revolution, the feeling of enmity was reserved for strangers. But the Industrial Revolution began separating people who previously felt closeness or amity. "A twelve-year-old child who works fourteen hours a day in a damp cotton mill is less likely to have the sense of 'belonging' than a farm labourer living in a small village," Wilson states.

In addition, during the Industrial Revolution, more of all kinds of products became widely available—including books and other publications. For the first time, people of all classes read. Authors such as Charles Dickens exposed the terrible conditions suffered by some members of society. Wilson says, "The denunciations of social injustice influenced every class of reader." Thus, people began to feel cynical, to have less faith in their society. The "age of enmity" began to grow, says Wilson.

Feelings such as longing for a better life, alienation (feeling separate) from society, and rejection by a society that no longer cared for and protected its members might have caused a "raging appetite that could turn to violence," Wilson states. He stressed, "Alienation tends to sharpen man's appetites." Wilson believes Jack the Ripper received a perverse thrill from the murders. At the same time, he got back at the society he felt had wronged him.

Victorian Attitudes

Since the victims were all prostitutes, the Victorians could not ignore the sexual aspect of the crimes. This was probably the most disturbing part of the killings. The Victorian era was a time of public and private repression of all things relating to sex. The

"Jack the Ripper was a homosexual sadist with a hatred of women."

Author and Ripperologist
Colin Wilson,
Encyclopedia of Murder

"These murders were committed by some person or persons who were perfectly sane."

Dr. Henry Sutherland,
a lecturer on insanity at the
Westminster Hospital,
September 1888

These prostitutes shamelessly showed their ankles at a time when the British people believed the human body should be completely covered.

idea of a sex crime was as horrifying as it was unimaginable.

Most people viewed sex as something that should be hidden, as should all things that could possibly be related to sex. The human body was to be covered at all times. To appear properly dressed in public, a lady or gentleman had to wear a hat to cover the head and gloves to cover the hands. Skirts and trousers were long enough to cover the tops of the shoes. Sleeves were long. Only the face was allowed to show. It was not unheard of to take a bath in underclothing or in a covered bathtub. Pregnant women had to go "into confinement" once their condition began to show. A proper lady did not leave her home or receive guests until after the birth of her baby. Language changed to accommodate the Victorian notion of modesty. Polite people no longer said "leg"; they said "limb." Even legs of tables and pianos had to be covered, and tablecloths came into fashion.

Naturally, prostitution was repulsive to the Victorian mind. It suggested the forbidden and encouraged men's baser impulses. Wilson writes that if Jack the Ripper had murdered nursemaids or housewives the public would have been shocked. But that he chose prostitutes "touched the deepest springs of Victorian morbidity." The crimes drew people's horrified attention to things they did not want to think about.

"A Sick Man"

Jack the Ripper "was a sick man, a man twisted with hatred and wracked by sadistic cravings," writes Wilson. He belonged to a group of people whose personalities are dominant—that is, they have to control other people. The Ripper had a need to dominate women. Wilson suggests that the Ripper was not a talented or creative man. He probably had no way to release harmlessly the overwhelming feeling that he must dominate a woman or kill her.

Probably Jack the Ripper was not very talented but was frustrated, angry at society, and maybe, suggests Wilson, a "downstart." A downstart is a person who works below his or her qualifications. For example, a downstart may be qualified to teach at the college level but can only find a job as a cashier in a grocery store.

With the opinions of Dr. Thomas Bond and Colin Wilson in mind, it is time to take a look at the suspects—and there have been many of them. Some have been poor and some wealthy, some have been laborers and some professionals, some have been cleverly calculating and some insane. One was a woman. And one was part of a Russian plot to discredit the British police! Here we will consider only a few of the best-known theories, keeping in mind a statement made by Kenneth Platnik, author of *Great Mysteries of History*. He writes, "The villain's identity remained a riddle. He excited the public imagination but never satisfied it. He deftly eluded every trap the police set, defied every effort to track him down." Is the Ripper among the people considered in this book?

Four

Who Were the Suspects?

The boxes of files compiled on the Ripper murders contain the names and descriptions of many suspects. Some can be easily dismissed because of lack of evidence. But many seem to fit the psychological descriptions Colin Wilson and others devised. Several are very similar in physical appearance, mode of dress, and personal background. All of the suspects have something disturbing about them. But which of them could have been the most compelled to commit the Ripper murders?

The Minor Suspects—Thomas Cutbush

Dr. Bond's 1888 report concluded that Jack the Ripper was a sex murderer. Thus, in 1891 when the police arrested Thomas Cutbush, the *Sun*, a newspaper, published a sensational article saying that the Ripper had been found at last. Cutbush was arrested for stabbing young women on the buttocks. He would assault his victims on public streets, always stabbing at them through their clothing. He took no further action against them.

Police Inspector Macnaghten reported that Cutbush "is said to have studied medical books by day, and to have rambled about at night, returning [home] frequently with his clothes covered with blood." But Macnaghten did not believe Cutbush was the notorious

Opposite: Despite the many clues Jack the Ripper sent the police, they never seemed to get close to him. Here *Punch*, a humorous newspaper, makes fun of the police's inability to catch the brutal killer.

Thomas Cutbush was arrested for assaulting women with a knife. But his crimes were on a much smaller scale than the Ripper's.

killer. For one thing, the evidence against him was questionable. The reports of his "bloody" activities were made by his "excitable" aunt and mother, and the knife he used on his victims was purchased long after the 1888 Whitechapel murders had occurred.

Most important, wrote Macnaghten, in the Whitechapel murders, "the fury of the mutilations *increased* in each case, and, seemingly, the appetite only became sharpened by indulgence. It seems, then, highly improbable that the murderer would have suddenly stopped in November '88, and been content to recommence operations by merely prodding a girl's behind some 2 years and 4 months afterwards."

Cutbush was eliminated from Macnaghten's list of Ripper suspects.

George Chapman

One of the most popularly held beliefs in Victorian England was that under no circumstances could a gentleman or an Englishman commit such a crime as the Whitechapel murders. Thus, many suspects were foreign. George Chapman was one of these.

Chapman was born in 1865 in a small Polish village called Nargornak. His real name was Severin Antonovich Klosowski. He studied surgery but failed to obtain his degree as a junior surgeon. According to author Donald Rumbelow, Klosowski worked as a hospital attendant or "barber surgeon." (This term was left over from the days when barbering and medicine were intertwined.) In 1888 Klosowksi emigrated to England, leaving a wife behind.

He worked in various shops in the Whitechapel area as a hairdresser's assistant. For a while he owned his own shop, but eventually it failed. He married again, although he never divorced his Polish wife. Unable to remain faithful to one woman, he lost his second wife as well. There followed a succession of

George Chapman, a Polish immigrant, was a favorite suspect with many who thought no Englishman could commit such ghastly crimes.

"You've got Jack the Ripper at last!"

Scotland Yard Inspector Frederick George Abberline to Inspector Godley on the arrest of George Chapman, October 25, 1902

"It is impossible to fit the two characters [Jack the Ripper and George Chapman] into the same frame, and on this ground alone Chapman should not be considered a candidate for the Ripper."

Author and Ripperologist Donald Rumbelow, *Jack the Ripper: The Complete Casebook*

mistresses. He took his new name, Chapman, from one of them.

In 1895, he set up housekeeping with Mary Renten Spink. Her husband, Alfred Spink, had left her and taken their child, because she was an alcoholic. Chapman and Mrs. Spink ran a musical barber shop together. She sang and he shaved. The money for the shop had come from Mrs. Spink's trust fund. The shop was amazingly successful, but the couple left it to become landlords of a tavern. Chapman continued to have other love interests.

On Christmas day in 1897, Mary Spink died after an illness of repeated vomiting and stomach pains. Chapman had nursed her, preparing her meals and medications.

Early in 1898, Chapman met Bessie Taylor. They also lived together as husband and wife and operated a tavern. In 1901 Bessie died of symptoms similar to those suffered by Mary Spink.

A few months later, Chapman met and set up house with a young woman named Maud Marsh. In the fall of 1902 when Maud became ill, her mother suspected that Maud was being poisoned. She called in a doctor to examine Maud. He wrote to a local doctor reporting that Mrs. Marsh was right. But the report was too late. Maud died the day after the examination, of massive poisoning. The post mortem showed traces of arsenic in her system.

Chapman was arrested on October 25, 1902. He was charged with the murder of Maud Marsh. The bodies of Mary Spink and Bessie Taylor were exhumed. Both were in excellent states of preservation, which, according to Rumbelow, "is an indication of poisoning by arsenic."

The arresting officer in the Chapman case was Inspector Godley. He had worked with Inspector Abberline on the Ripper investigation. Supposedly Abberline said to him, "You've got Jack the Ripper at last!"

George Chapman murdered several of his "wives."

Rumbelow summarizes some of the arguments in favor of Chapman being Jack the Ripper:

> that he was working in Whitechapel at the time and had the necessary surgical skill to have committed the killings and the mutilations both quickly and efficiently; that the description of the man who was seen with [Mary] Kelly was . . . an accurate description of Chapman; . . . the callous joking of some of the Ripper correspondence, which was typical of his brutal humor.

Rumbelow points out, however, that as with Thomas Cutbush, Chapman did not really fit the psychological profile of Jack the Ripper. Chapman murdered in a coldly calculating way. He systematically planned the poisoning of his "wives." He did not, like the Ripper, violently murder for the thrill of it. Rumbelow says that Chapman and the Ripper could not possibly be the same person.

Sir Arthur Conan Doyle proposed that the Ripper might be a woman, or a man disguised as a woman.

A killer disguised as a midwife or abortionist would arouse no suspicion.

Jill the Ripper

The author of the fabulously successful Sherlock Holmes stories, Sir Arthur Conan Doyle, created in Holmes the first "modern" detective. Holmes used brilliant deduction and scientific processes such as finger printing, tire tracking, and the identification of cigarette ashes to solve his mysteries. Doyle was asked who he thought Jack the Ripper might be. He responded that the murderer would have needed a disguise that would let him wander about the streets without arousing suspicion. Most likely, he said, that would be as a woman.

Some Ripperologists think that the Ripper was not merely disguised as a woman but *was* a woman. One such theory is discussed in Tom Collins' book *When London Walked in Terror.* Collins suggests that Mary Kelly was murdered by a prostitute friend who was jealous because Kelly chose to go back to living with her male friend. This theory, however, does not explain the other four murders.

Another Ripperologist, William Stewart, also believed the Ripper may have been a woman. Stewart used logical deduction to try to determine the class of person the Ripper might have been. The questions he asked were:

(1) What sort of person was it that could move about at night without arousing the suspicions of his own household or of other people that he might have met? (2) Who could walk through the streets in blood-stained clothing without arousing too much comment? (3) Who would have had the elementary knowledge and skill to have committed the mutilations? and (4) Who could have been found by the body and yet given a satisfactory alibi for being there?

Stewart inferred that this must have been a woman with a particular skill. He suggested that she was a midwife and an abortionist. The motive for the murders, he said, was perhaps that she spent time in prison after being betrayed by a married woman she had tried to help. (Performing abortions was against the law.) Consequently, she was "avenging herself on her own sex."

Rumbelow says that Stewart came by this premise because Mary Kelly was three months pregnant. She probably feared that she would be evicted from her room. So, Stewart suggests, she called the abortionist for her services, and Jill the Ripper took that opportunity to murder and mutilate Kelly.

The problem with this theory, says Rumbelow, is that none of the other victims were pregnant. They had been haggard, ill, middle-aged women. The midwife would not have been called for them.

Suspects with More Evidence Against Them— The Lodger

One of the best-known solutions to the mystery of Jack the Ripper was popularized in a novel called *The Lodger*, written by Mrs. Belloc Lowndes. The novel was serialized in a popular magazine and was later made into a stageplay and two movies. Mrs. Lowndes fictionalized information first published in a newspaper article about Dr. L. Forbes Winslow. He was a self-proclaimed "medical theorist and practical detective." Dr. Winslow stated to the *Times* that "the killer was a lunatic who had recently been released from an asylum or had escaped from one."

Winslow claimed that he had provided the police with information and methods to catch the killer. But they never pursued his ideas. Author Donald Rumbelow writes,

Forbes Winslow never doubted that if the police had acted on his suggestions then the police would have caught the Whitechapel killer. He was astonished that they did not appreciate their own incompetence and he was dismayed by their reluctance to allow others—himself—who were far more competent to handle the case, to take over the investigation.

"Jack the Ripper could have been a big, strong woman who had been engaged at a slaughter-house in cleaning up, and who also, now and then, had helped to cut up the meat."

London surgeon Lawson Tait, 1889. [quoted by Martin Howells and Keith Skinner in *The Ripper Legacy*]

"It is...extremely unlikely that Jack the Ripper was a woman for the simple fact that such psychopathic tendencies have always been virtually unknown in women."

Authors Martin Howells and Keith Skinner, *The Ripper Legacy*

Dr. Lyttleton Forbes Winslow was certain he knew how to catch the Ripper. The police, however, did not take him seriously.

(The police stated that they never received any information from Winslow beyond one unusual proposal to use warders from insane asylums to catch the killer.)

Winslow claimed that he could prove the identity of the murderer. He also claimed that he had stopped the Whitechapel murders. He based his claims on information he said he had gathered from detectives on the case, the lodging-house keeper where the killer had stayed, and prostitutes.

It was, in fact, a prostitute who gave him the first, most important clue. After the murder of what was thought at the time to be the Ripper's eighth victim, an unnamed prostitute told Winslow that she had seen a local lodger washing his hands at the back of a house in Finsbury. "The inference," writes Rumbelow, "was that he was washing off blood."

Mr. G. Wentworth Bell Smith

After investigation, Winslow found the lodger's rooming house. The lodger, Mr. G. Wentworth Bell Smith, was in London to raise money for the Toronto (Canada) Trust Society. The lodging-house keeper and his wife thought the man was odd. For one thing, he had an unusually large wardrobe for that time, and he often changed his clothes four times a day. He wore rubber-soled shoes, also uncommon, when he went out. He verbally abused prostitutes, saying they "should be drowned." He kept loaded guns in his room and acted suspiciously when anyone came to his room. The lodging-house staff thought he was dangerous. Also, he often stayed out late, creeping silently back into the house in early morning.

Winslow showed the *Times* reporter a pair of the rubber-soled boots. The tops were made of cloth and appeared to have great bloodstains on them.

The lodging-house keeper told Winslow that on one night when a prostitute was stabbed thirty-nine times, the lodger had come back to the house at four in the morning. When the maid cleaned his room, she

found that his bedding had bloodstains on it. She also
discovered a shirt with freshly washed cuffs.

Witnesses had described a man seen with Mary
Kelly. They had also given descriptions of men seen
near the scenes of two of the other murders. The
descriptions were remarkably similar, and the lodger's
appearance fit. He was about five feet ten. His hair
and skin were dark. He appeared to be unshaven but
well dressed. He, like the Ripper, carried a small
leather bag (as did many men in keeping with the
fashion of the day). In addition, the lodger had bragged
that he had performed fabulous operations, and one
woman claimed to have been accosted by him.

If Dr. Winslow's information was accurate, a lot
of circumstantial evidence points to the lodger as the
killer. Unfortunately, Dr. Winslow came by his
information more than a year after the last Ripper
killing, and he could find no trace of the mysterious

The young lodger seemed
sinister to his landlords.

Dr. Winslow said he saw the lodger's canvas-topped, rubber-soled, bloodstained boots.

Mr. Smith. Inspector Abberline claimed that he had never been given Winslow's evidence, and the police never sought out or interviewed the lodger.

The Slaughterman

Several experts, both from the time of the murders and today, believe that the dreaded killer must have been knowledgeable about anatomy and skilled with a knife. For this reason, surgeons have frequently been sought out as suspects. But there is another possibility. Perhaps the person was skilled in the dissection of animals, not humans. Perhaps he was a butcher of some kind.

Robin Odell wrote a book called *Jack the Ripper in Fact and Fiction*. Odell makes a strong case for the Ripper being a Jewish *shochet*, or ritual slaughterman. Such a killer would have suited the English sensibilities of the time better than an English gentleman would have.

A shochet is an educated man, devout in his faith. He kills sheep and cows according to the Jewish talmudic law so that the animals are *kosher*, or fit to eat. Using his very sharp knives, he slices an animal's throat to the bone with one quick, clean, back-and-forth motion. He cuts into the chest to examine the lungs and heart. He cuts into the abdomen to examine the stomach, kidneys, and other internal organs. All of the organs must be free of disease for the animal to be considered kosher.

Needless to say, he is highly skilled. A good shochet can complete his work on an animal in only a few minutes. Not only that, but he could do it without getting much blood on himself. According to a letter sent to the police by a butcher, a skilled butcher could kill a person in such a way that the blood would mostly flow into the ground and the victim's clothing.

Odell suggests that the killer could have been a psychopath suffering from a religious mania. "A ritual slaughterman steeped in Old Testament law might have felt some religious justification for killing prostitutes." Also, the shochet would hold a trusted and respected place in the community. He would have the confidence of the victims and would easily be able to lure them away. "In appearance, his dark clothes and black frock coat would have given him the slightly shabby and faded respectability that matched some of the descriptions of Ripper suspects," Donald Rumbelow writes. But no shochet was arrested and charged with the killings.

M. J. Druitt

Sir Melville Macnaghten stated that one of his great disappointments was that he became a detective officer "six months after Jack the Ripper committed suicide."

It is widely believed that Macnaghten was referring to Montague John Druitt. "Druitt is currently the firm favorite with most Ripperologists as the man most likely to have been Jack the Ripper," writes Donald Rumbelow.

Druitt was the second son in a large, well-to-do family. His father was a doctor. Montague Druitt earned a law degree after being educated in some of England's top schools. However, all did not go well for him. He was the kind of person criminologist Colin Wilson described as a downstart. His law practice never took off, so he supplemented his income by becoming a schoolmaster. In the fall of 1888, the fall the Whitechapel murders occurred, Druitt was dismissed in disgrace from his teaching position. The reason is not on record. However, some writers think it quite possible that he had inappropriate relations with students or that he behaved erratically. It is known that Druitt's mother had been institutionalized in July 1888, and he feared he too might be going insane.

Monday, December 3, 1888, was the last day Montague Druitt was seen alive. He visited his mother

"M. J. Druitt was sexually insane and from private information I have little doubt but that his own family believed him to have been the murderer."

Assistant Chief Constable Melville Macnaghten, in his notes on the Jack the Ripper case, 1894

"There was nothing seriously wrong with Druitt....My father, who was an experienced doctor, was quite convinced Druitt could not have been the Ripper."

A London doctor whose father went to Oxford with Druitt, quoted by Donald McCormick, *The Identity of Jack the Ripper*

According to one letter-writer, a butcher could easily have committed the Ripper's murders quickly and without much blood. A religious butcher, a shochet, might have had both the skill and the motive—ridding the city of evil women.

in the mental institution, filled his pockets with rocks, and threw himself into a river. In his pocket was a note reading, "Since Friday I felt I was going to be like mother and the best thing for me was to die."

Evidence Against Druitt

What kind of evidence links Druitt to the Ripper murders? Police Inspector Macnaghten wrote a lengthy note telling why he did not think Thomas Cutbush was the Ripper. In it he named Druitt as one of the three men he thought were much likelier suspects. He wrote that Druitt "was sexually insane and from private info I have little doubt but that his own family believed him to have been the murderer." Macnaghten never recorded what that "private info" was.

There is additional evidence that Druitt may have had reason to be in the Whitechapel area at the times of the murders. Varying reports say that his law office

was located there, that he had a cousin with a medical office in the area, and that he rented rooms in the area from time to time.

The police told the Vigilance Committee to cease its work shortly after Druitt's body was found. Apparently Macnaghten was not the only police officer to believe Druitt was the Ripper.

Walter Sickert, a painter we will hear more about in a later chapter, provided testimony to Macnaghten that Druitt was the killer. Sickert reported that his landlady told him that the previous boarder in his room was Jack the Ripper. She said that this boarder, a veterinary student, had acted very strangely. He often left at night and returned in the early mornings. The landlady found traces of his having burned his suits in the fireplace on the mornings after these late-night excursions. The boarder became ill about the time the

A newspaper artist's drawing based on one witness's description of the Ripper.

Montague John Druitt. After his 1888 suicide, the Ripper murders stopped.

landlady decided to warn the police. He was taken away by his mother to Bournemouth where he died three months later. This strange boarder was supposedly Montague Druitt.

Some of the details of this story obviously do not match the facts about Druitt. He was not a veterinary student. His brother, not his mother, lived in Bournemouth. And his mother was confined to a mental institution and could not have come to pick him up. Are these details proof that the boarder was not Druitt, or were they simply confused in the retelling of the story? No one knows.

According to Donald Rumbelow, the most convincing evidence is a report from a retired policeman, Steve White, who had spent many nights "loitering about the evil-smelling alleys of Whitechapel in search of Jack the Ripper." The policeman's description of a man he saw leaving the scene of one of the Ripper murders is extraordinarily like Druitt.

> I saw a man coming out of the alley. He was walking quickly but noiselessly, apparently wearing rubber shoes, which were rather rare in those days. . . . As he came under the wall lamp I got a good look at him.
>
> He was about five feet ten inches in height, and was dressed rather shabbily, though it was obvious that the material of his clothes was good. Evidently a man who had seen better days, I thought. . . . His face was long and thin, nostrils rather delicate, and his hair was jet black. His complexion was inclined to be sallow. . . . The most striking thing about him, however, was the extraordinary brilliance of his eyes. They looked like two very luminous glow worms coming through the darkness. The man was slightly bent at the shoulders, though he was obviously quite young---about thirty-three, at the most---and gave one the impression of having been a student or professional man.

A few minutes after seeing this man, Detective White heard another officer shout to him to come into the alley. There lay the bloody body of one of the Ripper's victims. When he ran back to the street to grab the man he had just seen, the suspect was gone, possibly hidden in one of the hundreds of lodging houses in the area.

Did the police officer have Jack the Ripper almost in his grasp only to lose him? Was the man Montague Druitt or only someone who resembled him?

As with the other suspects, the evidence is all circumstantial and open to interpretation. Druitt was insane—or thought he was—and he bore an uncanny resemblance to a man seen leaving the scene of one of the Ripper's killings. The killings did end after Druitt's death. Still, there is no existing evidence to prove beyond a doubt that Druitt was the killer. And there are still other suspects to examine.

The killer as described by one police officer. Was this Druitt?

"The London *Sunday Times* expressed belief today that Jack the Ripper, infamous London murderer of nearly 100 years ago, was Eddy, Duke of Clarence."

An Associated Press article from November 1, 1970, discussing conclusions reached by Dr. Thomas Stowell in *The Criminologist*

"None of the self-proclaimed witnesses who insisted they'd seen the Ripper near the scene of the crime ever mentioned a resemblance to Clarence. And on the dates of several of the slayings his whereabouts are listed and accounted for in the official Court Calendar."

Writer Robert Bloch, *Ripper!*

Royal Suspects

Prince Albert Victor, "Eddy," Duke of Clarence, was the grandson of Queen Victoria and her husband Prince Albert. Eddy had no royal responsibilities and no job to occupy his time. He was poorly educated and was known to philander away his energies with women and, allegedly, with men as well. In recent years, several writers have pointed to Eddy as the likely identity of Jack the Ripper.

First to make this accusation was Dr. Thomas Stowell. He wrote a sensational article in 1970 for the British magazine *The Criminologist*. He claimed as his source of information the private papers of Sir William Gull, the royal physician for Queen Victoria and her family. According to Stowell, Eddy had contracted syphilis while on military shore leave in India as a very young man. This disease often causes the health and sanity of its victims to degenerate dramatically. Stowell implied that Eddy had gone mad and become Jack the Ripper in the dark streets of Whitechapel. Certainly Eddy's physical description was similar to witnesses' descriptions of the killer and to many of the suspects. There was a particularly striking similarity between Eddy and M. J. Druitt.

Stowell did not directly identify the prince. He called him "S" in the article. And in fact, when asked, he denied that he was writing about Eddy. Still, says Rumbelow, the details he provided clearly fit the dissolute young prince.

Stowell claimed that the royal family knew of Eddy's vile pastime after the second murder, and perhaps even after the first. Stowell wrote that after the "double event" on September 30 they whisked Eddy away to a private mental asylum from which he later escaped to commit murder number five.

Another author, Frank Spierling, wrote a sensational book called *Prince Jack* in which he agreed with Stowell's views. Spierling claimed that

Dr. Gull had hypnotized Eddy and been horrified by Eddy's reenactment of one of the grisly crimes.

Despite these authors' claims, there seems to be more evidence that Eddy was *not* the murderer. For example, documents show that during two of Jack's murders, the prince was clearly elsewhere. On September 30 he was in Scotland shooting game, and on the day of the final murder he was attending his father's birthday celebration.

Despite these contradictions, Stowell's, Spierling's, and other versions do provide evidence that the prince may have been indirectly connected to the crimes. Michael Harrison, author of a biography of Eddy called *Clarence*, suggests that someone close to Eddy may have been the murderer. It may have been someone who wanted revenge against the prince or, quite the opposite, someone who wanted to protect him and the royal name. The most prominent of these suspects are James Kenneth Stephen, who was Eddy's close friend and tutor at Cambridge University, and William Gull, the royal physician himself!

James Stephen

Author Michael Harrison suggests that Stephen might have committed the murders out of a twisted desire to get back at Eddy after their friendship started to cool.

In 1883, Stephen, a bright and successful scholar, was appointed Eddy's tutor at Cambridge. The two young men became very close and spent much time together socially as well as at school. After two years, Eddy entered military service and the relationship gradually ended.

In 1887, Stephen was the victim of an accident that caused brain damage and ultimately led to madness. After his injury he became a patient of Sir William Gull.

Though impaired, Stephen held onto his ambition to be a writer. He tried his hand at publishing a small

Albert Victor, Duke of Clarence, known as Eddy. Note his strong resemblance to Montague John Druitt, shown on page 62.

Is it possible that Eddy, Queen Victoria's grandson, was the demented killer, Jack the Ripper? At least some evidence says he was not. On the date of one killing, he was hunting in Scotland.

weekly journal, but it failed after only a few weeks. Because of his injury and subsequent mental deterioration, Stephen became a downstart.

Stephen's poetry showed evidence of snobbery and hatred of women. In one poem, for example, he suggests of a woman he passed on the street, "She should be done away with, killed, or ploughed." Harrison finds this to be strong evidence that Stephen could have been the Ripper.

In addition, Harrison points out the similarity between the handwriting style of the Ripper's correspondence and Stephen's notes. In the letters from the Ripper which start "From hell" and "Old Boss," the *K* written by the Ripper is nearly identical to the way Stephen wrote his own initial *K*. In other letters, there is less similarity. Of course, as Rumbelow points out, it is not difficult to change one's style of handwriting.

Harrison also suggests that the style of Stephen's poetry is very similar to the verse in some of the letters allegedly written by the Ripper.

Finally, Harrison draws some very elaborate conclusions as to why Stephen's murders of five unknown prostitutes would disturb Eddy and thus be effective revenge for the loss of Eddy's friendship. According to Harrison, Stephen left obscure clues near or on the bodies relating to Greek mythology. Supposedly only Eddy would have understood their meaning.

Author Donald Rumbelow states that Harrison's theories are mere conjectures. They are not based on facts but on imaginings. If Stephen was the Ripper, the evidence certainly is not conclusive, he believes.

James Kenneth Stephen, tutor and close friend of Eddy. Did he commit the killings to get back at Eddy?

Dr. Gull

Another person close to both James Stephen and Prince Eddy is frequently mentioned as a likely Ripper suspect. He is Sir William Gull, physician to Stephen and the royal family. Gull became the Royal Physician when he cured the Prince of Wales, Eddy's father, of typhoid fever. In gratitude, the Queen appointed Gull her Physician Extraordinary. He was also the Physician in Ordinary to the Prince of Wales and the royal family generally. When Eddy was suspected of insanity, Gull was the attending physician.

Dr. Gull was seen in Whitechapel on more than one of the evenings the Ripper murders occurred. This is not surprising, says Thomas Stowell. Gull's papers indicate he was there to certify "S" as insane and wanted to observe his behavior. Rumbelow, however, does not agree that this was a valid reason for Gull to be there. He points out, "It is hardly necessary to catch 'S' in the act of murder to prove his insanity."

At the time of the murders a spiritual medium named R.J. Lees had visions foreseeing the Whitechapel murders. In his first vision he saw the murderer. The murderer wore a dark tweed suit and a light-colored overcoat. Lees believed he used these to cover up the blood stains on his clothes. That very day Lees saw this same man on a bus. The police did

Dr. William Gull, physician to the royal family and a suspect in the Ripper case.

not believe Lees's story, and the man got away. Lees later identified the man as Dr. Gull.

In Lees's second vision, he saw the mutilation of ears, just as happened in the Chapman murder. The police were surprised, because Lees described this vision to them before the mutilation was reported in the newspapers. But it was Lees's third vision the police took most seriously. He foresaw the killing of Mary Jane Kelly in Miller's Court.

Because of Lees's extraordinary vision, the police used him to trace the whereabouts of the killer. Author Stephen Knight reports that Lees's greatniece told him that Lees guided the police to the home of a famous doctor. The doctor's wife supposedly admitted her husband had sudden "manias for inflicting pain." He had tortured the family cat and brutally beaten their son. The doctor had been out on the nights of the murders. His wife could not say where.

Was Dr. Gull a respectable physician by day and a murderer by night?

Psychic Robert James Lees identified Dr. Gull as the killer.

Seeking the Killer

The doctor admitted under questioning that he had memory losses since a stroke some months before. When the police interviewed him, he had scratches on his face and bloodstains on his shirt. He had no explanation for them. The police found clothes similar to those Lees had seen in his vision.

Knight writes that the distressed doctor wanted to commit suicide. Instead, a committee of distinguished doctors committed him to an insane asylum where he died many years later. Was this man Dr. Gull, and was he the mad killer?

Thomas Stowell does not think so. He believes that the doctor showed the police a bloodstained shirt in an attempt to draw attention away from Prince Eddy. Although Donald Rumbelow does not accept Stowell's implication that the prince was the killer, he does agree that most likely Gull was not. Rumbelow reports,

> Medically the slight stroke that Gull had in 1887 was the first attack of severe paralysis. Although he recovered from it, its effects were serious enough to prohibit him from further medical practice. Taken with the fact that he was seventy years old at the time, this is surely enough

GHASTLY MURDER

IN THE EAST-END.

DREADFUL MUTILATION OF A WOMAN.

Capture ┋ Leather Apron

Another murder of a character even more diabolical than that perpetrated in Buck's Row, on Friday week, was discovered in the same neighbourhood, on Saturday morning. At about six o'clock a woman was found lying in a back yard at the foot of a passage leading to a lodging-house in a Old Brown's Lane, Spitalfields. The house is occupied by a Mrs. Richardson, who lets it out to lodgers, and the door which admits to this passage, at the foot of which lies the yard where the body was found, is always open for the convenience of lodgers. A lodger named Davis was going down to work at the time mentioned and found the woman lying on her back close to the flight of steps leading into the yard. Her throat was cut in a fearful manner. The woman's body had been completely ripped open, and the heart and other organs laying about the place, and portions of the entrails round the victim's neck. An excited crowd gathered in front of Mrs. Richardson's house and also round the mortuary in old Montague Street, whither the body was quickly conveyed. As the body lies in the rough coffin in which it has been placed in the mortuary —the same coffin in which the unfortunate Mrs. Nicholls was first placed—it presents a fearful sight. The body is that of a woman about 45 years of age. The height is exactly five feet. The complexion is fair, with wavy dark brown hair; the eyes are blue, and two lower teeth have been knocked out. The nose is rather large and prominent.

to cast doubts on the story of his roaming about Whitechapel trying to catch his patient. There is enough internal evidence in the story to show that the doctor referred to could not have been Gull. According to Lees, the wife complained that she had caught her husband brutally beating their small son; Gull's son by that time was a Barrister [lawyer], and so could hardly have been the child referred to. Finally, Gull did not die in a lunatic asylum. He died at home on 29 January 1890, after a third stroke which left him speechless.

Nevertheless, Gull is a prominent suspect in another author's theory that will be explored in the next chapter.

More Questions

Did Jack the Ripper murder and mutilate prostitutes for insane gratification as Colin Wilson and others suggest? Or is there more to the story? Could the whole Ripper reign of terror have been an elaborate political cover-up?

"The slight stroke that Gull had in 1887 was the first attack of severe paralysis. Although he recovered from it, its effects were serious enough to prohibit him from further practice."

Author and Ripperologist Donald Rumbelow, *Jack the Ripper: The Complete Casebook*

"Gull's constitution had not been impaired by serious illness. All his life he was remarkably healthy."

Author and Ripperologist Stephen Knight, *Jack the Ripper: The Final Solution*

Opposite: A broadsheet (a large, single-sheet newspaper) sold on the streets during the Ripper scare. At this point, the main suspect was a man known as "Leather Apron."

Five

Were the Whitechapel Murders a Political Cover-Up?

Opposite: The Ripper murders may have had a political motive. This cartoon shows what many officials feared during Queen Victoria's administration: that the poor would revolt, the'queen and her administrators would lose their power, and anarchy (an absence of government) would reign.

During the hundred years since the Whitechapel murders took place, most theories about the murderer have concluded that a single madman perpetrated the crime. That one man has been called Jack the Ripper.

But in 1975, a book appeared called *Jack the Ripper: The Final Solution*. Its author, Stephen Knight, argues against the theory that one man committed the horrendous Whitechapel murders. Knight insists his research proves Jack the Ripper was not one man but three. The murders were not committed by a man seeking sick sexual gratification. The crimes were an elaborate political cover-up. The list of those involved, Knight contends, included the queen herself. Although Knight's research and evidence are contested by some prominent Ripperologists, they are interesting enough to examine in some detail.

The Doctor and the Coachman

The story of a political conspiracy involving Dr. Gull and others was told to Knight by a man who

Walter Sickert, a prominent painter and friend of Eddy. Was Sickert involved in the coverup of Eddy's politically unwise marriage?

claimed to be the son of a painter named Walter Sickert. Sickert had a shop across the street from the male brothel supposedly frequented by Prince Eddy and James Stephen. Author Stephen Knight interviewed the son, Joseph Sickert, at length. Sickert told him that Gull was the Ripper and that he was aided by a coachman named John Netley. They committed the crimes to protect the royal family from scandal.

Sickert said Eddy often spent time at the artist's studio. There he met and fell in love with a girl named Ann Elizabeth Crook who worked nearby. She became Eddy's mistress, then his wife. The marriage took place in secret in 1888. Ann Elizabeth was Catholic, and Eddy would have been prevented from marrying her because of strong anti-Catholic feeling at the time.

Supposedly Gull and other high officials found out about the secret marriage and a baby born to the couple. They conspired to find a way to end this disgraceful union without the public ever knowing about it. Gull was chosen to carry out this plan because of his closeness to Eddy.

Knight reports that Ann Elizabeth was abducted and confined in a hospital where her mind was destroyed. But this was not enough. Mary Kelly had witnessed the marriage of the prince and the Catholic girl. She too had to be silenced. To save the honor of the throne, Gull and Netley killed her. The other Ripper victims were killed for one of two reasons: either to distract the police and public from the real motive, or because Mary Kelly and three of her friends were attempting to blackmail the royal family with their knowledge.

The Political Climate

Why would such a drastic solution to a royal indiscretion have been needed? After all, members of the royal family were often featured in the scandal sheets of the day, without causing a revolution.

According to Knight, Queen Victoria's government was in a fragile position. Her critics claimed that since the death some years before of her beloved husband and counsel, Prince Albert, Queen Victoria had been an ineffective monarch and ruler. Her country experienced neglect. The poor suffered and the rich profited.

Not only did the queen pay less attention to her duties than many felt she should, but her son Edward, the heir apparent, was held in great disdain by the people of the realm and by the queen herself. Edward, the Prince of Wales, says Knight, had an odious reputation. The prince's own coachman was reported to have said, "God will never allow such a wicked man to come to the throne." This statement expressed the opinion of the common people only too clearly.

Some experts thought Victoria would be the last monarch. Socialism was becoming widely popular. Republicans and social reformers began to cry out for a change. Every unsavory, politically unwise move made by members of the royal family was published in the day's scandal sheets.

Knight writes, "Poverty and disease ravaged the lower class no worse than they had in previous reigns, but thanks to the Republicans, now the poor had someone to blame—the idle rich." And, in fact, on November 13, 1887, a year before the Ripper murders

Queen Victoria. Some say the queen knew the Ripper's identity and may even have been involved in covering up his crimes.

On Bloody Sunday, poor people demonstrated in Trafalgar Square. The queen's soldiers violently brought them under control. Some of the queen's advisers were afraid this kind of event would become commonplace.

"Everything Walter Sickert had said about Prince Eddy, Annie Elizabeth Crook, Sir William Gull and the murders themselves were true. . . .It is clear from the depth and accuracy of his knowledge that Walter Sickert knew more than he claimed."

Author and Ripperologist
Stephen Knight, *Jack the Ripper: The Final Solution*

"Whichever way you look, there is not a shred of evidence to back up Knight's theory; there's absolutely nothing to connect. . .Walter Sickert with the Jack the Ripper murders."

Author and Ripperologist
Donald Rumbelow, *Jack the Ripper: The Complete Casebook*

began, many of London's poor revolted. On Bloody Sunday, the poor who hung out in Trafalgar Square in central London clashed violently with the police.

They protested their anger at the unfairness of their treatment by the greatest empire on the face of the earth. When they worked, they shouted, they were so underpaid they were unable to care for their families. When they were unable to work, their lives were unbelievably miserable.

The Expendable Poor

Certainly the public was not unaware of the hardships these people endured. A popular pastime for the rich was to go "slumming": to patronize a poor shop in the East End, to take a food basket to a poor family, or to volunteer at the local parish. It was also a well-known habit of some of the wealthy gentlemen to visit the prostitutes of the East End where they could not help but view the extreme conditions of poverty. Still, industry exploited the poor for cheap labor on the docks, in the garment factories, and in other sweatshops. The poor felt as though they were an expendable class of people for the nation, and for the royal empire, to exploit.

By the autumn of 1887, trying to survive an already very cold season, the poor were outraged. Nobody should have been surprised at the confrontation.

Bloody Sunday, combined with other rumblings of discontent, made some of the queen's advisers uneasy about the future of the monarchy. The hope was that the young, attractive Eddy would help regain the people's support. But, says Knight, Eddy unfortunately followed in his father's dissolute footsteps. Public knowledge of his marriage to a Catholic would have been the last straw for those who were already discontent. According to Knight, Robert Salisbury, the queen's prime minister, knew of Eddy's marriage, and he knew it must never be publicized.

To prevent the downfall of the throne, he tried to find some way of covering up the situation.

Knight says that Salisbury was not only concerned about the monarchy. A powerful secret organization to which he belonged and which had a major influence in the ruling of the country could also find itself exposed and ruined if this scandal came to light.

Many of England's top politicians, artists, and thinkers were members of this group, the Freemasons. Among them were Walter Sickert, the painter who became friends with Eddy and at whose house Eddy met his bride; Sir William Gull, the royal doctor; and Inspector Abberline, who collected, wrote up, and maintained most of the records on the Ripper killings.

One bit of suspicious evidence suggesting a conspiracy, according to Knight, is the condition of the police files on the killings: The first two murders, of Nichols and Chapman, have volumes of paper. There are reports of every kind, from the notes of the first police officer on the scene, to forensic evidence, to police interviews, to lengthy notes of the post mortems and inquests. But as the killings continued, instead of showing more evidence, the files became slimmer and slimmer, until the fifth murder, of Mary Kelly, which has very little of consequence recorded in the police files.

Robert Salisbury, Queen Victoria's prime minister. He was also a Freemason. Was he involved in a Ripper conspiracy designed to save the throne and the Freemasons?

A Freemason event in which the Mason directly to the left of the table is being disciplined for something he has done. Note the many Masonic symbols worn by the men and engraved on the walls.

Author Stephen Knight says that Eddy secretly married a Catholic girl and that Mary Kelly, one of the Ripper's victims, was a witness.

Knight suggests that someone "got" to Abberline. Says Knight, it was as if he knew who the Whitechapel murderer was—and he knew Jack the Ripper was not going to kill again.

Mary Kelly

As mentioned previously, Mary Kelly had supposedly witnessed the wedding of the prince to the Catholic girl, Ann Elizabeth Crook. One version has it that she told three friends (Mary Ann Nichols, Annie Chapman, and Elizabeth Stride), also prostitutes, the story. Together they decided to blackmail the authorities. But whether Mary Kelly alone knew of the wedding or whether she told others, she had to be silenced, says Knight.

Salisbury called upon Sir William Gull to rid them of Mary Kelly. Knight suggests that Gull "was possessed of a bizarre sense of humor" and "created"

Jack the Ripper to assure that "the reins of power were to remain firmly in Masonic hands."

The Plot Begins

On August 31, the systematic plan began with the murder of Mary Ann Nichols in Buck's Row. A week later Annie Chapman was disposed of. Then Elizabeth Stride met Jack the Ripper on the night of the double murder on the thirtieth of September. Catherine Eddowes was butchered in Mitre Square that same evening. But Gull had made a mistake, says Knight. Eddowes had also gone by the name Mary Kelly. The real Mary Kelly had to be found. The community of London and all of England cowered in fear as she must have done. If indeed three of the Ripper's victims were her friends and blackmailing co-conspirators, she had to have known she would be the next victim.

On November 9, 1888, Jack the Ripper found Mary Kelly in Miller's Court. Afterward, he disappeared forever, without a trace.

The Freemasons

Who were the Freemasons, the powerful and secret organization that might have initiated such a terror? Originally, they were the guild for architects that was formed during the Middle Ages, a sort of "primitive trade union," says Knight. These architects, the stonemasons and bricklayers, were the builders of the European cathedrals and other massive structures. They had a specialized craft they felt needed to be protected from outsiders. They established "lodges" to which employers and employees belonged. "Lodges all over agreed to adopt secret signs, passwords, and handshakes so that a mason coming to a strange place would be recognized by his brothers as a genuine craftsman," says Knight.

As the centuries passed, this secret society of Freemasons evolved into a social organization. The fraternity accepted all professionals. Knight writes, "By the eighteenth century, Freemasons were, in

"Jack the Ripper was at large and might strike again at any time. But the Yard obviously knew something, or they would not have been content to let the allegation reports build up without taking any action to investigate suspects."

Author and Ripperologist Stephen Knight, *Jack the Ripper: The Final Solution*

"The police could have known (or at least suspected) the killer's identity but were ethically constrained to reveal his name after his death. This, however, does not seem likely."

Authors Martin Howells and Keith Skinner, *The Ripper Legacy*

A Freemason ritual.

practice, linked to their skilled predecessors only in name and in the form of their ritual." The Freemasons had become a "quasi-religious secret society."

The Freemasons have perpetuated many myths about their beginnings. These include the construction of the great buildings of the Roman Empire, the Great Pyramid of Giza, Noah's Ark, the Tower of Babel—and the most sacred of all, Solomon's Temple. Masonic secret ritual is based on that building.

The secrets of the society are protected by the threat of death in case of betrayal by a brother. Knight says, "An initiate swears on pain of death and ghastly mutilation to obey not only the precepts of Free-masonry but also those of the Bible and laws of the land in which his Lodge operates. . . . Having passed what is known as the Royal Arch [the highest level], a mason owes his allegiance only to his brother Masons." In this highest degree a Mason will swear even to murder and commit treason to protect the brotherhood, says Knight.

He says that the highest ranking Freemason in England at the time of the Whitechapel murders was Sir Charles Warren, the commissioner of the Metropolitan Police. Knight believes Warren secured this position because of his ranking with the Masons. Knight suggests that Warren's appointment was solely to aid in the concealment of facts during the murders. Knight states that Warren asked for the resignation of non-Mason James Munro, head of the Criminal Investigation Department (CID), just before the murders began. Warren appointed a high-ranking Mason, Robert Anderson, as Munro's successor on the eve of Mary Nichols' murder. Both Warren and Anderson had reputations as woefully inadequate police officers. Anderson fled for Switzerland the day after his appointment. Continually throughout the investigation of the murders Warren destroyed, lost, or dismissed evidence. Finally, "Warren disappeared from the scene only hours before the murder of Mary Kelly."

Masonic Evidence

Knight says there is specific evidence that connects the Freemasons to Jack the Ripper. Here are some of the points he cites:

First, Freemasonry makes use of many symbols and rituals. In one of the rituals an intiate mimes the result of betrayal: In the lowest degree, the penalty for revealing the secrets of the Brotherhood is to have the throat cut from left to right. The victims of the Ripper all had their throats cut from left to right.

Second, the mutilations of the Ripper's victims are remarkably similar in each murder. They have "extraordinary parallels with the ritual killings [prescribed by] Freemasonry," says Knight.

Third, Knight contends that Jack the Ripper is really three people: Gull, Netley, and Sickert. For the Freemasons, three is the perfect number.

Fourth, at the scene of at least one of Jack's crimes was a curious array of clues that appeared to have been left deliberately: Annie Chapman was found with two brass rings, two new farthings (coins), and a few other items laid out at her feet. Knight explains:

Top: Sir Charles Warren. Bottom: Sir Robert Anderson. Both of these men were Masons, and both were known as less-than-excellent police officers. Were they involved in a plot to save Freemasonry and the royal family from the anarchy of the poor?

Annie Chapman's body was found surrounded by several items significant to Freemasons.

The act of placing brass rings and other items by the body was Masonic, in an act of twisted symbolism. Brass is the sacred metal of the Masons . . . . [because of] two great hollow brass pillars which stood at the entrance to Solomon's temple, and which have become the symbol of Freemasonry . . . . The other more obvious Masonic aspect of the episode is that before a Mason is initiated to any degree he is divested of all metals such as coins and rings.

The rings were missing by the time Annie Chapman's body was in the mortuary. The cover-up was already in play, says Knight. He suggests that Dr. Phillips, the attending coroner, took the rings. Phillips was a Freemason.

Fifth, the presence of the cut-off leather apron at Annie Chapman's murder scene, Knight suggests, is also symbolic of the Freemasons. Many craftsmen wore such aprons to hold the tools of their trade. Thus, the leather apron was an important symbol to the Masons.

Sixth, Knight even sees Masonic symbolism in the time periods between killings. The number of days, at least between the double murder and Kelly's murder, has special meaning to Freemasons.

Seventh, if Gull had not made a mistaken identification, the final, culminating murder—that of Mary Kelly—would have been a grandly symbolic event to all Freemasons. Due to Gull's error, the victim was Catherine Eddowes, not Mary Kelly. Still, the symbolic effect was the same. Mary Kelly was to have been murdered in a Masonic ritual fashion. Eddowes, murdered and mutilated, was placed in Mitre Square. "The mitre and the square are the basic tools of the Freemason," wrote Knight. And, "they play a large part in Masonic ritual and allegory." Additionally, Mitre Square was named after Mitre Tavern, "an important meeting place of the Masons." Dr. Gull's own lodge, the Royal Alpha, used the Mitre Tavern as one of its frequent meeting sites.

Eighth, after Eddowes was found in Mitre Square, a piece of blood-soaked apron was discovered lying in a nearby street passage. On the wall above the apron was written:

The words written on the wall near Catherine Eddowes's body.

> The Juwes are
> The men That
>   will not
> be Blamed
>   for nothing

Suspiciously, Commissioner Warren forbade a photograph of this evidence. And at his order the message was wiped out. He stated that he had had the message erased to protect the Jewish community. But Knight contends that Warren's master was not justice but the Higher Degree of the Masons. What he tried to do was cover up the meaning of "Juwes." It is not a misspelling of "Jews." It is the name of three

Stephen Knight believed he had sufficient evidence to show that Dr. Gull, driver John Netley, and painter William Sickert committed the Ripper murders together.

assassins in Masonic history who are the basis of Masonic ritual, says Knight. This message is the final and most clear link connecting the Freemasons to the Ripper murders.

Dr. William Gull

Suppose that Knight is correct about the Freemasons being the source of a murderous conspiracy. What evidence does he have to link Dr. Gull to the murders? Many people say that a man in his seventies, who had also suffered a stroke, could not be strong enough to walk the streets of the East End, let alone murder and mutilate women.

Knight proposes that Gull suffered only a mild stroke. There is on record testimony that he was a man of incredible strength. Knight insists this man was not impaired by his so-called stroke.

And even if he was weakened, he was not a lone assassin, says Knight. His accomplice or accomplices could have held the victims as Gull performed the rituals. The accomplices, Knight says, could have been a coachman, John Netley, and the painter Walter Sickert. Netley had often driven Eddy around the Whitechapel area; he could have driven Dr. Gull. Netley, says Knight, was most eager to serve the Masons well in order to advance his own fortune. He could have lifted and carried the bodies. Gull need not have expended much energy. Sickert, as an artist, knew much about anatomy and about the princely scandal. Knight says that there were numerous "artistic" touches at the murder scenes that could have been Sickert's doing. And he points to several of Sickert's paintings that seem to hint at inside knowledge of the killings.

The Evidence

Knight's evidence for Gull's involvement includes the following: Gull was a Freemason. He suffered from attacks of mental illness, at which time his behavior was strange and often violent. He had been seen in Whitechapel on the nights of at least three of the murders. He had strong anatomical knowledge and surgical skill. The morning after one of the murders, according to his wife, he had woken with blood on his clothes which he could not explain. There was also, of course, the evidence of Joseph Sickert, Walter's son, who, says Knight, claimed Gull was the killer.

Sickert and Knight were not the only ones who thought Gull was Jack the Ripper. Knight cites a newspaper article from the *Chicago Sunday Herald* of April 28, 1895. This article does not name Gull, but speaks of a highly prominent physician from the West End of London. It says this doctor was brought before a secret commission on charges of lunacy and was thought to be responsible for the Ripper murders. The information on which this article was based came

Dr. William Gull at his writing desk.

After the Ripper murders began, the ladies of Whitechapel began carrying various protective devices. Unfortunately, they were not enough to save Jack's victims.

READY FOR THE WHITECHAPEL FIEND. WOMEN SECRETLY ARMED.

from a Dr. Howard who said he was a member of the secret commission. From the details in the article, Knight believes the doctor was William Gull.

Opposing Views

What do other Ripperologists think of Knight's detailed theory that Jack the Ripper was not a single madman but a conspiracy designed to protect the English throne and the power of the Freemasons?

Donald Rumbelow, for one, thinks it is a fantasy. If Walter Sickert knew so much, he asks, why was he allowed to live and to continue painting, even leaving clues about the murders in his art? The goal of such a murderous conspiracy would be to eliminate all possible threat of exposure of Prince Eddy's indiscretion. Mary Kelly and four other prostitutes were killed. Dr. Gull was confined to a mental asylum. Why would Walter Sickert be allowed to live free and unhindered?

Rumbelow contends that Knight makes up "facts" or changes them to suit his purpose. He also points to a statement by Joseph Sickert, Knight's chief source of information. Two years after the publication of Knight's book, Sickert renounced it, saying that he had made up the story he told Knight. Knight, in turn, renounced Sickert's statement. He said Sickert was probably just having a change of conscience at seeing his father connected in print to the crimes of Jack the Ripper.

Another Ripperologist, Melvin Harris, author of *The Ripper File* and *Jack the Ripper: The Bloody Truth*, says that Knight's theory is "spurious." He points out that Joseph Sickert has admitted he made up his entire story. Harris says,

> All competent research confirms this. Until [Sickert] named Gull and Netley as partners in the killings no one *anywhere* had ever dreamed of such a deadly alliance . . . . As things stand, an honorable man and an outstanding physician has been branded a killer . . . . The public has been duped.

Harris has his own favorite candidate for Jack. He nominates a single villain named Robert D'Onston Stephenson. He believes Stephenson, also known as Roslyn D'Onston, performed the murders as part of a Satanic plan.

Who is right? Who was Jack the Ripper? Author Donald Rumbelow writes, "I have always had the feeling that on the Day of Judgment, when all things shall be known, when I and the other generations of 'Ripperologists' ask for Jack the Ripper to step forward and call out his true name, then we shall turn and look with astonishment at one another as he announces his name and say: 'Who?' It will be someone unknown or unsuspected by the scores of Ripperologists who have studied the crimes."

Conclusion

The Search Goes On

Were the Ripper murders the crimes of a sick and perverted killer? Were they a cry for attention to the horrible living and working conditions of the poor of London in that late-Victorian era? Were they a political cover-up?

Donald Rumbelow writes, "One of the things that I have learned about playing the game of 'Hunt the Ripper' with correspondents from all over the world is that every fact is capable of being wrenched into the weirdest of interpretations." And indeed, much of what has been written about this most notorious of killers has been denounced by other "experts" as being a "twisting" of the facts.

The Ripperologists who travel to London to do their research find that time—more than one hundred years have passed since the killings took place—is only one of their enemies. The police files are frustratingly incomplete. The newspapers of the day often did not report straight facts. They embellished in order to excite the interest of their readers. Did the London police of 1888 solve the mystery of Jack the Ripper and then suppress the answer? If they did not, can we hope to solve it today?

Many people think we can. In recent years, several television programs have documented the murders,

providing their own solutions. Dozens of books have been published, each with its author's own "final" solution. Perhaps one of these will give us the answer to the mystery of who Jack the Ripper was.

Bibliography

Paul Begg, *Jack the Ripper: The Uncensored Facts.*
London: Robson, 1988.

Tom A. Cullen, *When Terror Walked in London.* New
York: Houghton Mifflin Company, 1965.

Daniel Farson, *Jack the Ripper.* London: Michael
Joseph, 1972.

Melvin Harris, *Jack the Ripper: The Bloody Truth.*
London: Columbus Books, 1987.

Melvin Harris, *The Ripper File.* London: W. H.
Allen, 1989.

Stephen Knight, *Jack the Ripper: The Final Solution.*
Chicago: Academy Chicago Publishers, 1986.

Donald McCormick, *The Identity of Jack the Ripper.*
London: Arrow Books Ltd., 1970.

Robin Odell, *Jack the Ripper in Fact and Fiction.*
London: Harrap & Co., 1965.

Donald Rumbelow, *Jack the Ripper: The Complete
Casebook.* Chicago: Contemporary Books, Inc.,
1988.

Andrew Sinclair, *Jack: A Biography of Jack London.*
New York: Harper & Row, 1977.

Frank Spiering, *Prince Jack.* New York: Doubleday
& Co., 1978.

Lytton Strachey, *Queen Victoria.* New York: Har-
court, Brace & Company, 1921.

Index

Picture Credits

Mary Evans Picture Library, 11, 18, 20, 39, 46, 49, 65, 67, 69, 75T, 75B
Courtesy of Melvin Harris, 13, 23, 24, 26, 27, 29, 30, 33, 35, 36T, 36B, 56, 61, 70, 73, 74, 77T, 81T, 81B, 83, 86
The Bettmann Archive/Hulton BBC Library, 15, 16, 19, 28, 32L, 42, 44, 54T, 66, 77B, 80, 85
The Mansell Collection, 17, 41, 68T
Popperfoto, 32R, 51, 62, 87
Amy Johnson, 50, 53, 54B, 57, 58, 60, 63, 68B, 78, 82, 84

Acknowledgements

Thank you to all these people for sharing their talent with me: To Cleone for clarifying the dream. To Bruno for saying yes. To Terry O'Neill for being a tremendously helpful editor. To Anne and Lucas, Cathy and Katie, Holly and Kelly, and Jennie for proofreading for me. To the librarians of Weyauwega and Fremont, Wisconsin, and Bedford, Indiana, for helping with the research. To Dad, Bec, Chris, and Greg, my wanna-be-writers-too. To Bill for loaning me Hal. And to Nick and Madelaine for loving me.

About the Author

Katie Colby-Newton earned a B.A. in Elementary Education from the College of St. Catherine and an M.A. in Religious Studies from United Theological Seminary, both in St. Paul, Minnesota, Katie's home town. Presently Katie is living in Bedford, Indiana, with her husband William and children Nicholas and Madelaine. Although she loves to write, Katie is the first to admit that she reads far more than she writes. She says, "I read everything. Cereal boxes, novels, short stories, articles, newspapers, labels on cans. . . ." Her other interests include recycling, painting landscapes, and visiting art galleries and museums.

Jack the Ripper is Katie's first book in the Great Mysteries series. She believes the story is more than a mystery. It is a tragedy that ruined far more lives than those of the five women killed by the elusive butcher.